Canada Goose
in flight

THE COTSWOLDS ILLUSTRATED TOWN & VILLAGE GUIDE

The Crab Apple.

BY

COTSWOLD ARTIST

PETER REARDON

HERB ROBERT

FROG

1

Published by
REARDON PUBLISHING
PO Box 919, Cheltenham, Glos, GL50 9AN.
Website: www.reardon.biz

Cinnabar Moth
and catapillar

Cat Black and Yellow

Written and Illustrated
by
Peter T Reardon

Emperor Dragonfly

Book Design by
Nicholas Reardon

The front cover shows different parts of Bisley

Three-spined Stickleback

Minnow

ISBN 9781901037098

This book is dedicated to the memory of a great
Cotswold artist

"Peter Reardon"

Many people will remember seeing Peter's work not only in many
Cotswold books, but also as regular features in many local newspapers.

This book you are holding your hands is not only a great guide to the
Cotswolds, but a real product of this wonderful part of England, as it has
been written, illustrated, designed, and published all within the Cotswold
area.

The Cotswolds

The beauty of the Cotswolds is not new. It is not something that has just come about recently. It is, you might even say, as old as the hills themselves. To the visitor from other parts, it has a unique splendour all it's own. To those fortunate enough to live here, it is seen in a different way.

Through the ages this beauty has been captured by the artist's brush, the pen of the writer and in more recent times, the camera lens of the photographer. There are many fine paintings in existence of the great country houses in wonderful settings, and much has been written of the towns and villages of the Cotswolds. But it is not only beauty to be found in these hills, they are rich in history also.

The Romans came, stayed a while and then left. They were about the first to leave us monuments of their advanced way of life that we can understand today. Then came the Saxons, the Danes and the Normans. Each left something by which to remember them. In more recent times great houses have been built and are there for all to see, each giving something to history and in particular, the Cotswolds. Some of these features have been included in this book, so that you can be acquainted in words and pictures, with but a few of the details that make up the wonderful story of these hills.

The Cotswolds   intriguing, majestic, even cruel in its own way. There is a bigness that is breathtaking, especially during the summer, a loneliness that can be frightening during the winter, but always a grandeur, as powerful as an exciting tale that not one little bit must be missed. Perhaps early man found the excitement of these hills a good reason for settling in them. They offered a natural fortification in many instances for settlements, often with views over the valley of the Severn, where animals could be hunted and fish caught in the river. There were also numerous small rivers which offered fish, water and game.

It is hoped that your visit to the Cotswolds will be most enjoyable, and if, with the help of these pages, more memorable, then the object of this publication will have been achieved.

Do come again.

PETER T. REARDON

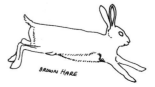

BROWN HARE

Acton Turville

A quaint little village at the junction of the B4039 and B4040. Just over a mile to the north is Badminton Park. Which was built in the latter half of the 17th century. On the south east corner of the Park is a long barrow called the Giant's Cave. It has been excavated twice, once by an Edinburgh team who took all the remains back to their museum. It was, unfortunately, damaged during road reconstruction. Three big stones remain in the centre and it seems possible that there was a dry stone wall surrounding the tomb. On the right is a picture of the Well at Acton Turville, and it will be seen that the portcullis emblem is also found in the Coat of Arms of the Dukes of Beaufort.

Amberley

Set on the western slopes of Minchinhampton Common at about 550ft. Amberley overlooks the Nailsworth Valley towards Woodchester Park on the other side. Just a small gathering of various buildings, among them

Rose Cottage. Mrs. Craik, who wrote the novel "John Halifax, Gentleman", lived here and much of the story included Amberley and Rose Cottage under different names of course. "Abel Fletcher's Mill" at Tewkesbury, some twenty miles north (as the crow flies) on the A38 was also the scene of many doings in the tale. The little drawing on the left shows a monument erected to commemorate Queen Victoria's reign in June, 1897. It can be seen at the cross roads in the village opposite the Inn. Up on the common above Amberley there is plenty of room for ball games with the family or just plain walking. For those interested in archaeology there are a number of features to be seen some dating back nearly 3,000 years.

4

Bath

A city with a long history, much of which is still visible today. Once the Roman town of Aquae Sulis, the site has been known to men much earlier than this, probably due to the finding by ancient man of the hot springs that come up from the ground. This is the only place in Britain I know where there is natural hot mineral springs gushing from the earth. Bath, the name we know it by today, is perhaps one of the oldest cities in the country, a great deal having been done to preserve not only its buildings but it's character as well. Many celebrities have lived or stayed in Bath at some time or other including Royal visitors, but the city owes as much to the three men, Beau Nash, Ralph Allen and John Wood as anyone. Beau Nash (real name Richard Nash) was a gambler from London and having won much money from people in Bath found a strong affection for the town. He brought Fashion and Society to Bath, which in turn brought money thus helping the city to prosper. With the help of Ralph Allen, postmaster and quarry owner many new and impressive buildings were erected to the designs of John Wood, technician and architect. Below is a view of "Sham Castle", a folly built by Ralph Allen of Bath stone from his quarry.

Sham Castle

5

Bath

Beckford Tower

As a city, Bath is not big, and some beautiful and interesting walks can be enjoyed in a short distance.

The picture to the left shows the Beckford Tower at Lansdown. At one time the private retreat of William Beckford, a wealthy man of many roles.

There is every amenity here for the visitor no matter what their liking museums, galleries and exhibitions for those who want to know, shops and restaurants, wonderful gardens to sit in and soak up the sun and sports of all kinds for the energetic ones. A major attraction of course, is the famous Roman Baths near the Abbey. Bath is a must for everyone visiting the South Cotswolds.

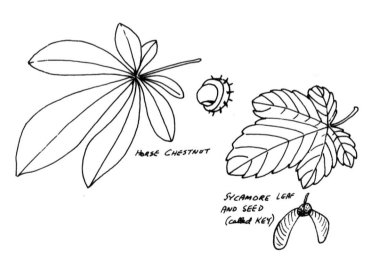

HORSE CHESTNUT

SYCAMORE LEAF
AND SEED
(called KEY)

Berkeley Castle

In the Vale of Berkeley, part of the Severn Valley, lies Berkeley Castle, formidable and awe inspiring. Its history is closely linked with the Cotswolds and for this reason it is felt that it should be included in this little book. The Castle has been occupied by the Berkeley family right through from when it was built in the 12th century to the present time. At the time of the Civil War, 1642-9, much damage was done to the Castle, including breaching the west wall of the keep.

The gatehouse

The gatehouse shown is at the car park entrance on the B4066. Edward Jenner, best known for his discovery of vaccination came from the town of Berkeley. For a short time he lived in Cheltenham, but returned to Berkeley in later years where he died.

Near the Castle can be found the famed Jenner museum and his cottage, the museum is well worth a visit, and it is a must to see the little building like a retreat which he used as a surgery for treatment. His tomb is in the church just across the way.

The Church is St. Mary's where you can also find the tomb of ill-fated Dicky Pearce, the last Court Jester in England and who died in Berkeley Castle by falling from the Minstrels Gallery.

Bibury

This must surely be one of the most unchanged villages in the Cotswolds though one of the most frequently visited.

The church, acquired by the Monks of Osney, was partly rebuilt on the site of an earlier building. A number of architectural periods in the fabric are of some interest, as are the cast of an Anglo Saxon tombstone dated around 1000 AD, the original being held in the British Museum. Tombstones in the floor of the nave go back to 1700 and a brass plaque on the chancel arch is to the memory of Frederick George, 5th Baron of Sherborne and Vicar of the parish for 42 years. On the outside a good Norman doorway can be seen in the north wall, also a stone, believed to be a tombstone of early Saxon times built into the north wall of the Chancel. This little feature is shown in the drawing on the left.

Bibury

The Bridge over the River Coln in Bibury leads you to the delightful Arlington Row built in the 15th century.

ARLINGTON ROW — BIBURY.

Bisley

A village lying about 3 miles east of Stroud and has many features to offer the visitor to the Cotswolds. The little sketch shows part of the Seven Springs of Bisley. The water comes from natural springs and has not been known to dry'up. Each year, a ceremony called Well Dressing takes place on Ascension Day when the children dress up for this special occasion. Its origins probably go back to pagan worship. In those days it was believed that to pacify the water spirits ensured a constant flow from the springs, this being very important to the local people of the day as there was no piped water to supplement it. The church has many interesting relics for the visitor to browse over, some going back as far as Roman times. The churchyard is not without its interest too, maybe foremost being a monument, hexagonal and with a spire surmounted by a cross. The structure shown on the next page is supposed to cover an ancient well, the legend being, that after a local priest had fallen into it and drowned, the well was sealed up.

AN 'OLD WORLD' CORNER of BISLEY IN GLOUCESTERSHIRE

REARDON

Bisley

Bourton on the Water

Much favoured by tourists from all over the world, Bourton on the Water has quite a variety of interests to offer. The Model Village is a must when visiting Bourton, and can be seen in the grounds of the Old New Inn. It is of course, a model of Bourton on the Water. Birdland, with a diversity of species in all their magnificence of colour is an attraction which thrills young and old alike, and one that should not be missed. Art galleries form part of the scene of Bourton with their air of sobriety, paralleled only by that of the museums. At the Perfumery, it is possible to sample some of the wonderful perfumes actually made and blended on the premises. The Motor Museum really is different. An interesting assemblage of some old favourites, also Britain's largest collection of signs associated with motoring. Afternoon teas with homemade cakes are to be enjoyed at several pleasing tea rooms offering their services.

The Motor Museum

12

Bourton on the Water

The drawing above shows the last bridge you will see when leaving Bourton on the water.

Bourton is on the famous Fosse Way, or A429 as we know it today. The drawing below shows the skull and crossbones over the west door of the Church of St. Lawrence.

Bretforton

The charming fleece Inn in the village of Bretforton after being in the same family for over 500 years it is now in the safe hands of the National Trust.

"THE FLEECE INN" AT BRETFORTON, Nr EVESHAM.

MARBLED WHITE BUTTERFLY

BRIMSTONE BUTTERFLY

and Caterpillar

SMALL WHITE Butterfly

14

Broadway

This wonderful Cotswold town has many fine examples of old stone houses dating from the 17th and 18th century.

The picture on the next page shows a large tower standing on a spot known as Broadway Beacon, right on the edge of the Cotswold escarpment above the town of Broadway. It was built by the Earl of Coventry for his Countess, who wondered if a fire built on this spot could be seen from their family home at Croome Court. It could be, so the tower was built and from the top the views on a clear day are breathtaking, and must surely be one of the finest viewpoints in this part of the country.

Broadway Tower is reached by turning south off the A44 Broadway to Moreton in Marsh road at the top of Fish Hill, which overlooks Broadway. The lane adjacent to the tower follows part of Buckle Street, one of the old Roman Roads.

Broadway Tower

Broadway Tower

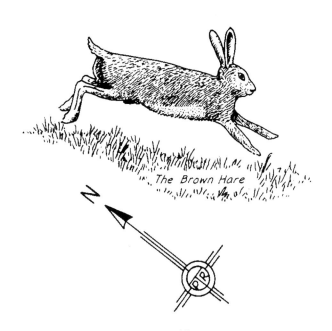

The Brown Hare

Burford

Although in Oxfordshire, Burford is popularly known as "The Gateway to the Cotswolds".

There is much here to interest the visitor to this town with its historic buildings and, pictured here above, the Tolsey. At the north end of town is a fine example of a packhorse bridge while in the High Street are many good Inns and coaching houses. The town has very early associations with transport and travel and, lying on the River Windrush as it does the name was possibly derived from burn, meaning stream and ford, meaning crossing. Burford is situated on the north side of the junction of the A40 Cheltenham to Oxford and London road with the A361 Chipping Norton to Swindon road.

The bridge over the River Windrush at burford

18

Castle Combe

One of the lovely and unspolit villages of England, Castle Combe nestles in the wooded valley through which flows the little By Brook.

In the 1960's people with all kinds of equipment invaded the village to make film sequences for the movie "Dr. Doolittle', and the cottages, bridge and stream at the southern end of the village became a fishing harbour overnight. Not surprising really that Castle Combe was selected for this role as it was once claimed to be the prettiest village in all England. The little drawing shows the old stone Market Cross with the pump still by its side, unfortunately not now in working order, and with what is known as the Butter Cross just on the left of it.

Chalford

Christ Church, in an Alpine Setting at Chalford

Known as the Alpine Village of the Cotswolds, Chalford lies on the northern slopes of the Golden Valley overlooking the River Frome. Christ Church from high ground with the other side of the Golden Valley looking towards Minchinhampton. The old Severn and Thames Canal flowed through this valley from Framilode on the Severn, to join the Thames at Lechlade via a 2¼ mile long tunnel at Daneway, Sapperton.

The picture to the right is of natural springs known as the Tankard Springs, and have never been known to run dry. They can be found in the High Street not very far from Christ Church. Opposite the church is a Round House once used by lengthsmen on the canal.

20

Cheltenham

An excellent centre from which to tour the Cotswolds and a beautiful town in itself. A Regency style Spa with fine hotels, shopping centre second to none, lovely parks and gardens, all set in elegant tree lined roads at the foot of the Cotswold Hills overlooking the Severn Valley and Welsh mountains.

Cheltenham is famous for its Spa Waters, discovered in 1718 by, not a man, but pigeons. Hence the pigeons in the Town's coat of Arms. After George III's visit to the town in 1788, it became the fashionable thing to come to Cheltenham Spa and partake of the mineral waters. It is an interesting fact that these springs produce the only natural alkaline Spa Water in the country fit for human consumption. The little drawing on the left shows one of the urns found in the Town Hall which once held the Cheltenham spa waters for people to drink. Over the page you will see the famous "Devil's Chimney" landmark over looking Cheltenham.

Cheltenham

The DEVIL'S CHIMNEY. CHELTENHAM.

REARDON.

Cheltenham

Cheltenham is noted for its fine public buildings, shops, colleges and by no means least its churches. Pictured here below is the magnificent 15ft. Rose window to be found in the north transcept of the famous Parish Church of St. Mary, right in the centre of Cheltenham. The church spire is visible from several points in the town but because it is surrounded by tall shops and buildings, the church cannot be seen from the road. Due to this seclusion an air of tranquillity reigns making it a place to pause for a moment and collect oneself. Inside the church, the impression of space and grandeur somewhat belies the external appearance. The colour in the finely traceried windows and the exquisite carving of a screen in the south transcept and chancel add to the wonder of this place of worship. The walls are rich in tablets and brasses of celebrated people who have lived and died in and around Cheltenham.

Chipping Campden

Famous the world over, Chipping Campden boasts architectural gems in the Cotswold style unchanged for hundreds of years.

The Market Hall, of which a view through an archway is shown here, was built in the 17th century by Sir Baptist Hicks. Although a London merchant, Sir Baptist chose to live at Chipping Campden and had a beautiful mansion built close to the church. It was, unfortunately, mostly destroyed during the Civil War and only a handful of remains exist today. The gateway still stands though not complete. Sir Baptist Hicks was also. responsible for the building of the Almshouses near the church, perhaps the most popular place in Campden for artists and photographers. Sir William Grevel, wool merchant and benefactor of the town, leaves his home as a memorial to those days of wealth.

Chipping Norton

This pillar shown can be seen behind the Town Hall in Chipping Norton. The stone at the base of this column formed part of the old wayside cross removed from near this spot before the building of the town hall. The upper part is one of the nine pillars of the old market which stood here until 1842 when it was removed so that the present Town Hall could be built.

FERAL PIGEON

Chipping Sodbury

Almost at the southernmost part of the Cotswolds lies the "Sodburys". They are a group of three, Chipping, Old and Little. Just after World War 11, Chipping and Old Sodbury were formed into one Parish and today, they are, geographically, one town. The history of the Sodburys goes back to before Roman times and many interesting discoveries have been made. In the picture on the right below shows a clock tower above a building. The clock was originally a memorial to Lt. Col. George William Blathwayt of Dyrham Park, some four miles south of Chipping Sodbury. In later years an addition in the form of public conveniences was made around it, and then finally a concrete shelter with seats was added in more recent times. It now also serves as the local bus stop, and tourist information. The Sodburys lie on the A432 near the junction with the A46 Bath to Stroud to Cheltenham road, about 3 miles north of junction 18 of the M4 Motorway.

Cirencester

A town that has figured in the history of the country, county and Cotswolds since it was just a settlement of the Boduni tribe. When the Romans invaded Britain for the second time, they marched over the Cotswolds to a spot where they came across this settlement, and it was here that they built a fortress which was to become the foundation of the town of Corinium. (the town we know as Cirencester). The picture below shows the remains of the Hospital and Chantry of St. John the Evangelist, in Spitalgate Lane, which was founded by Henry 11 in the 12th century. So, too, was a great abbey only to be destroyed some 400 years later at the Dissolution of the Monasteries in 1539. All that is left now is what is known as the Spital Gate (from Hospital Gate). This gateway was probably built by the early English learning much of the art of building from the Normans. Of much later date is the Barracks at Cecily Hill shown over the page, in a quiet niche away from much of the towns bustle near the very imposing gates of Cirencester Park. The Park is open for visitors to the town to enjoy walks and picnics. One of the features to be found in the Park is a little structure called Pope's Seat, a kind of summer house where the poet, Alexander Pope, used to be a frequent visitor.

Cirencester

Barracks at Cecily Hill

A town with something to suit most tastes, Cirencester has a long and interesting history. The town grew under Roman rule as an administration centre, being situated at the junction of Ermine Street, the Fosse Way and Akeman Street. Being second only in size and importance to London.

There is an excellent museum of Roman remains in the town, a testimonial to the high standard of work and living of those times. Many of the roads today follow the routes of the old Roman Imperial Posting Roads like part of the A417 and the A429. The route of the Fosse Way can be travelled by major and minor roads nearly all the way to its end at Lincoln. Construction of these great roads, which were built mainly for military purposes, was basically similar to the way ours are built today. First the direction of the road was sighted out by the Roman engineers, the construction gangs following in their wake digging out the foundations and either driving in heavy timbers end on or placing very large stones as a base. A layer of cemented big stones was followed by a layer of gravel or small stones mixed with cement and topped with large flat stones cemented in position. Edging stones were built up to contain the fabric of the road to the full depth.

(CROW FAMILY)
ROOK

Coates, The Round House

In the early 1800's the Severn & Thames Canal was operating to carry bulk goods from Bristol to London. To help pay for the upkeep of the canal, tolls had to be collected. This was done by dividing the canal up into sections and toll keepers living in round houses similar to the one shown in the sketch, could collect their dues from the boats as they went from section to section. To prevent boats slipping past without paying, a stout chain was drawn across the canal at these points just under the water line. The remains of the round house shown can be found about a mile SW of the village of Coates on the south bank of the canal. Much work has been done on this part of the canal including restoring the south portal of

the tunnel. Coates lies about 4 miles west of Cirencester just south of the A419, Cirencester to Stroud road.

Compton Abdale

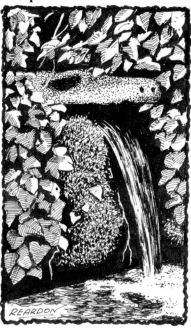

In the Cotswolds, springs have always been looked upon with some reverence, possibly because at one time it was the only source of local water. These springs gush forth from odd places, each being individual in their own way; a muddy pool at Thames Head not far from Cirencester, recessed wall at Chalford, canopied outlet at Shipton Oliffe, ornate design for 7 springs at Bisley, pictured here on the left, the bizarre, the head of a crocodile. This head can be found at the road junction in Compton Abdale just close to the church. Compton Abdale lies about 5 miles west of Northleach on the south side of the Northleach to Oxford road. The crocodile head has been the object of many a motor club treasure hunt.

Compton Abdale

- COMPTON ABDALE -
· GLOUCESTERSHIRE. -

Cricklade

A little old town with a lot of history behind it straddling the Ermin Way, or A419(T) as we know it today, about 7 miles SE of Cirencester. Cricklade, lying in a large area of flat agricultural land just over the border into Wiltshire, is the first town on the River Thames. History has involved the town since the days of the Romans, and in the cemetery can be seen a part of a wall, believed to be a fragment from Saxon times when there was a wall and ditch form of defence. The Severn and Thames Canal passed half a mile away at the north end of town but is now unfortunately derelict. The little drawing on the right shows the town clock at the junction of the B4041 and B4040, just off the A419. It is a well known landmark to travellers of the old Cirencester to Swindon road.

Daglingworth

A small village 3 miles north of Cirencester just to the west of Ermine Way, the A417. The Church of The Holy Rood will of course, provide much of the interest for the visitor to Daglingworth. There is much that is old, with examples of Roman, Saxon

and Norman work. Over the doorway to the porch is a sundial of Saxon origin, one of the finest in the country. Near the church, there is, as shown in the little sketch above, a circular type of dove cote with a revolving ladder inside to enable the 500 nesting boxes round the wall to be reached.

Didbrook

Nestling under the western escarpment of the Cotswolds lays the little village of Didbrook. A mile along a footpath to the south are the ruins of the once great Hailes Abbey. The Church, that of St. George, featured in the Wars of the Roses. In 1471, the Battle of Tewkesbury took place, but the widespread slaughter was not confined to around Tewkesbury. Apparently,

a handful of Lancastrian soldiers sought refuge in the little church at Didbrook. This was, however, to no avail for they were discovered by the Yorkists, put against the oak door and shot. It is claimed that this is one of the first times that hand guns were used in this country. The Abbot of Hailes Abbey, who was also the Rector of St. George's at Didbrook, was so distressed at this desecration that he had the church torn down and rebuilt at his own expense. It is strange, but whether by design or for any other reason the church is unique in that there is neither a north or south door, just a single west door. Much material from the old building must have been used in the new one', since the bullet marks from that day are still in the old oak door.

Duntisbourne Abbots
The 13th Century Church of St. Peter in the Cotswold village of Duntisbourne Abbots

Duntisbourne Leer
Showing a picturesque corner of Duntisbourne Leer

A PICTURESQUE CORNER of DUNTISBOURNE LEER IN GLOUCESTERSHIRE.

Duntisbourne Rouse

A very small village nestling on the hillside overlooking the River Dun. The main feature of the village is perhaps the little Church of St Michael, with Saxon as well as Norman work. The location of the church, on such a steep bank as it is, made easy the building of a crypt beneath the chancel. In itself not unusual, even in small Cotswold churches, but to have a footpath and doorway at crypt floor level is almost unique. In a recess just by this door is a stairway that led to the Chancel but is now sealed up. From the picture of the Church from the churchyard, the slope of the ground can be seen. The doorway to the crypt is not visible because a large tomb is in the way. Once through the lych gate and along the grass walk, access to the churchyard is through a slatted wooden gate. There is an interesting scissor type Iron Gate right

alongside, allowing one person at a time to go through. Duntisbourne Rouse is only a mile north of Daglingworth.

Dursley

Nestling on the slopes of a promontory of the western Cotswold escarpment, Dursley is perhaps a suitable place from which to start for some very pleasant walks and rambles. The town is still very quaint with its old buildings flanking steep winding little streets. The Church of St.

James dates from about the 15th century, and the Market House, opposite was built in 1738. A statue of Queen Anne, high up on the east wall of the Market House is shown in the sketch on the right. Dursley lies on the A4135 Tetbury to the A38 road, about 4 miles from Cambridge (Glos) and 13 miles from Tetbury.

Evesham

The building shown here is the entrance to the famous Almonry Museum in Evesham, at one time the residence of the Almoner from the Abbey.

Town Stocks outside the Almonry Museum

Near St Lawrence Church is the Remains of the Norman Gateway to the Abbey precincts, the gateway is actually the lower part of the building through which people can walk, the halt timbered part being built much later.

Norman Gateway to the Abbey precincts

Fairford

A picturesque town truly Cotswold. The Old Mill pictured at the bottom of this must have been a familiar sight to many of our American allies who were stationed here during the '39 '45 War.

Famous for its 28 painted windows is the 15th century Church of St. Mary, shown in the distance across the field and River Coln. The Mill is now a private residence. John Keble, who was educated at Corpus Christi College, Oxford, and became professor of poetry at 39, was born in Fairford in 1792. Keble College, Oxford, was built in his memory in 1870. The Town is well provided with inns. Pictured right is the best of the Cotswold tiler's craft with its variations in

direction and angle of slope. This example above shows the back of The Bull as seen from the A417.

THE OLD MILL -
FAIRFORD.

Filkins

Above and on the right is another cotswold lock up, this time in the village of Filkins, just over the border in Oxfordshire. Not much room inside for one person, never mind two. The chains, and what looks like a massive bear trap would not be conducive to a restful night, especially during the summer. The opening in the door is only about six inches square so ventilation was limited, and only the spout of a pot could be got between the iron bars across the hole if the prisoner wanted a drink. On the opposite page is the Lamb Inn only a few short steps from the lock up described above. It's possible that the reveller, starting in the Lamb, finished up in the Lock up. Filkins, once the home of the late Sir Stafford Cripps and Lady Cripps, has benefited much by their benevolence. They presented a Hall and Centre to the village, constructed by local craftsmen using local materials. After the death of Sir Stafford, Lady Cripps moved to Minchinhampton. Filkins can be found on the east side of the A361 about midway between Burford and Lechlade in Gloucestershire.

The Four Shires Stone

This large monumental looking structure can be found nearly 2 miles to the east of Moreton-in Marsh on the A44 Chipping Norton road. It marks a spot where some years ago the boundaries of the four counties of Gloucestershire, Oxfordshire, Warwickshire and Worcestershire used to meet. In 1935 the county boundaries were adjusted and Worcestershire does not now meet here, the nearest point of this county boundary being about 5 miles due west of Moreton in Marsh at a place called Spring Hill House.

35

Frampton Mansell

In the area of Gloucestershire called the Golden Valley you will discover this lovely church of St Lukes

THE CHURCH OF ST LUKES at FRAMPTON MANSELL IN THE 'GOLDEN VALLEY' GLOUCESTERSHIRE

Gloucester

Gloucester, the county town, has a history going back to before Roman times. When they came they made Glevum, as it was known then, into a military stronghold. The Saxons came and in the 7th century established a monastery which the Normans restyled in the late 11th century, when the Cathedral was built. This is almost all that remains of the once great Abbey of St. Peter, due to the Dissolution in Henry VIII's time. The small sketch shows the 13th century King Edward's Tower by the Cathedral. This City is well worth a visit from anyone coming to the Cotswolds, as there are attractions to suit everyone, from an up to date Shopping Centre to the revitalised Victorian Docklands of Gloucester.

KING EDWARD'S TOWER

36

Gloucester

GLOUCESTER CATHEDRAL from the SOUTH WEST

This picture shows the Cathedral flanked by the warehouses in Gloucester Docks. Ships up to 1000 tons can still be accepted in this, the most inland port in the country, via the august Gloucester and Sharpness Canal.

Hailes Abbey

The little drawing on the right does not really portray the grandeur associated with the ruins of something like an Abbey. It does however; show the excellent state of preservation of some of the details to be found. The section shown now covered for safety is part of the drainage system of the old Abbey, having continuously running water. This was probably supplied from a spring starting near Little Farmcote on the hills above, the water course being diverted to the Abbey then flowing on to the River Isbourne which joins the Avon at Evesham in Worcestershire. Hailes Abbey lies about a mile off to the right of the A46, 2 miles north of Winchcombe on the road to Broadway.

37

Hawkesbury Upton

On the right is a drawing of the Somerset Monument standing some 650ft. above sea level overlooking the village of Hawkesbury Upton. About 120ft. high, there are 144 steps to reach the platform at the top. It was erected in memory of General Lord Robert Somerset, the fourth son of Henry, 5th Duke of Beaufort. His remains were interred in St. Peter's Church in Hanover Square. The monument was designed by Lewis Vulliamy and built in 1846. Lewis was born in Pall Mall in 1791, exhibited many designs at the Royal Academy during his life and died in 1871. The Church of St. Mary in Hawkesbury has much to interest the visitor here both inside and out. Mostly 15th century, there are some earlier remnants. At the road junction in Hawkesbury Upton is an old pump and cross, the pump being used up to the war time when mains water was laid on.

Hetty Pegler's Tump

Half way between Dursley and Cainscross just off the B4066 is the village of Nympsfield. Nearly a mile north west of the village is the Nympsfield Long Barrow, twice excavated, the second time just before World War II. It is now, fortunately, in the care of the Dept. of the Environment. 400yds to the south of Nympsfield Long Barrow is Coaley Peak. From here wonderful views can be obtained. Car parking, picnic area and nature walks are available so there is lots of fun for all the family. A mile south of Nympsfield Long Barrow is Hetty Pegler's Tump, a burial mound and chambers in good condition. Two of the five chambers have been sealed off because they were considered unsafe. The plan of both barrows is similar. On the left is a little drawing showing the entrance to Hetty Pegler's Tump. Half a mile south again is Uleybury hill fort, an iron age camp site some 3000 years old covering almost 40 acres, the best in the country.

Kingswood

A little town just over a mile south of Wotton under Edge, on the B4060. At one time a place of some importance, a great Cistercian Abbey having been built here by the Normans. At the Dissolution in Henry VIII's time most of it was pulled down leaving only the lady chapel as a church for local people. In the early 1700's this was subsequently cannibalised to provide material for a new church that was to be built.

The picture to the left shows the abbey gate house, all that is left of this great house of God.

Lechlade

The little bridge pictured here on the right carries the A361 Burford to Swindon road over the River Thames at Lechlade. Built in 1792, it was at one time a toll bridge, when a halfpenny had to be paid before a traveller was allowed to dross to the other side. The toll keeper lived in the house attached to the bridge as shown in the drawing, and the upkeep of the bridge and house was paid for by the tolls collected from the wayfarers.

This bridge lies south of Lechlade and about half a mile from where the old Severn and Thames canal joined the Rivers Thames and Coln. At this junction one of the old Round Houses, built for the lengthsmen on the canal, still exists in good condition and is occupied.

The Long Stone

Woodchester, Avening, Bisley are names of places near Stroud where antiquities seem to abound. They are there for all to see, each having its own story to tell, but they must be looked for and all but the casual observer should be able to find them. Such a one is illustrated on the right and is known as the Long Stone. The legend surrounding this stone is that it had strange healing powers, especially where the disease of rickets is concerned. In medieval times, a newborn child would be passed through the hole in the stone, as it was believed that by doing so the child would be protected from the malady for the rest of it's life. The stone is large, about 8 ft. high, and stands in one corner of a field just off the road. If the road is taken from Minchinhampton to Avening, the Long Stone can be found in the field on the left hand side just before the hamlet of Hampton Fields.

Lower Slaughter

Just a few miles from Bourton on the Water is the village of Lower Slaughter The large sketch shows the river Windrush and the Lower Slaughter Mill, which was once the bakery for this part of the Cotswolds. Here one can see a village which is still unspolit by the relentless tread of the 20th century.

Lower Slaughter is easy to find being just off the Fosse Way between Bourton and Stow on the Wold.

Malmesbury

Old, in fact very old, is this town of Malmesbury, dating back to about the 5th century. Its religious origins evolved around the late 600's, culminating in a beautiful abbey being built during the Norman period. The door and porch can be seen on the south side, and has some of the finest carving perhaps in the world today, there being about 75 pictures from the scriptures carved on a series of stone bands running right round the door. Fortunately, the entire structure was not razed at the Dissolution, the nave and porch being left standing and serving as the church to this day. Near the junction of the A429 and A434 stands the 15th century Market Cross, shown in the picture on the right. Described as expensive at the time of building it was also useful for holding market on wet days.

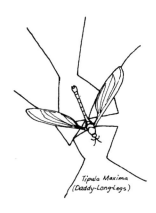

Tipula Maxima
(Daddy-Long-Legs)

To the left a view through the ruined part of Malmesbury Abbey

Minchinhampton

The MARKET HOUSE
at MINCHINHAMPTON GLOS

REARDON

The Market House, built in 1698 is still used today. The Church of the Holy Trinity is worth a look while in town, and over the page our main picture is of the Cross in the Market Square, Minchinhampton.

Tom Long's Post

Minchinhampton

— The MARKET SQUARE.
MINCHINHAMPTON —

REARDON

Probably, best known for the common (N.T.), nearly 600 acres of land. The small drawing on the previous page is of Tom Long's Post at the junction of six roads on the common, in memory of Tom Long, highwayman, who took his own life at that spot rather than be captured. Also one can see Iron Age earthworks called the Bulwarks and an Iron Age Camp fort at Amberley. A Long Barrow, damaged, is at the north end. There is a golf course and plenty of room for family fun and games or just for walks. The town has many fine buildings which owe their existence to the great days of wool in the 17th century.

Morton in Marsh

To the right we have a nice illustration of the war memorial in Morton in Marsh again another St George slaying his foe the Dragon.

Morton in the 17th century used be called "Morton Hindmost" and at another time "Morton Henmarsh"

The bottom picture is of a nice peaceful spot in Morton and a memory of past times as near by the busy main road you will discover the towns Duck pond

Tufted Duck

Nags Head

This little hamlet lies a mile east of Avening on an unclassified road to Cherrington. The drawing shows a decorated panel on the front of the old inn. Not all decoration, it does serve a useful purpose, that of bee hives, access to them being from an upstairs room.

A short distance away to the north is Aston Down airfield when, during right conditions, gliding can be watched. 3 miles north west is Minchinhampton, an old wool town with its Market House of 1698, a fine example of this kind of building. Holy Trinity Church has interest outside and in its contents, there being memorials to many local gentry.

Nailsworth

Reclining in a valley about 4 miles south of Stroud, Nailsworth has its associations with the wool trade of the Cotswolds.

After turning left at the Clock Tower, (Pictured on the next page) the first turn right goes up to Minchinhampton via the Devil's Elbow, and the second turn right is the way to the Common by way of either Nailsworth Ladder, or the Double U, (both old pack horse trails and later used as Motor Club trials hills), and the village of Watledge. Nailsworth straddles the junction of the A46 Cheltenham to Bath road and the B4014 Malmesbury/Tetbury to Nailsworth road.

THE CLOCK TOWER
NAILSWORTH, GLOS

REARDON

Northleach

Shown here is the picturesque old world Sherborne Arms set overlooking the Square in Northleach. Made wealthy and famous by the wool merchants of the middle ages, the town has changed little, and there is no doubt this little house of refreshment has witnessed many a good and bad deal, both on the market square and within it's walls. Although now renovated and taking in the adjoining forge as a restaurant, none of the charm has been lost in so doing.

— THE PICTURESQUE 'SHERBORNE ARMS' AT NORTHLEACH, GLOUCESTERSHIRE.—

PEAKLEY.

While in Northleach, a look at a house of a different kind would be interesting a house of detention. Built 400 years ago it is unfortunately now just a relic of the past. Not very comfortable, but larger than some that are still about, the dweller never stayed long. Usually a day and a night was the term and this was decided by the Northleach Court Leet, which was the local government of the day. The Northleach Court Leet is still active today. The Lord of the Leet is Earl Bathurst, whose family has held this position as far back as the Dissolution of the Monasteries. Today, the High Steward summons 12 men to meet on a specified day in November, to hold court as has been done through the centuries. There is a written constitution of 39 laws which can still be enforced since they have never been repealed by any government up to now. It was these laws, and probably others besides, that put people in this little place.

Northleach

The Old Lockup below is to be found in a corner of the Market Place, right by the Post Office. In those days there was a market cross where the War Memorial now stands in the opposite corner of the square to the Sherborne Arms. The Northleach Court Leet has records going back to the 16th century, with entries like 'John Proffyt was fined 6/8d. because wife tooks lbs of butter 'ere the Market Cross', and 1638, a record of 6 pence being paid for faggott to burn deceased pig.

the Old Lockup   *the Tyndale Monument*

North Nibley

Best known for the Tyndale Monument on Nibley Knoll. If one's pleasures involve rambles, scenery and history then there is much enjoyment to be gained around Nibley. The little drawing above shows the Tyndale Monument, viewed from the B4060 Dursley to Wotton under Edge road. Erected in 1866 in memory of William Tyndale, the English writer who, in 1525, produced his translation of the New Testament. He was burnt at the stake in Antwerp, Belgium, in 1536 for being a heretic. It was built here because it is believed he was born at North Nibley. Standing 650ft. above sea level overlooking the Severn Valley and Welsh Mountains to the west, the structure is 100ft. From the M5 Motorway. the Monument can be seen for about 13 or 14 miles from north of junction 15 to half way to Gloucester.

Notgrove

A view encompassing the unspolit village of Notgrove

NOTGROVE, AN UNSPOILT VILLAGE NESTLING IN THE COTSWOLD HILLS of GLOUCESTERSHIRE.

Painswick

A small Cotswold town, famous most, perhaps, for its churchyard with 99 yew trees. It is said that the 100th will not grow, but if it does another dies soon. Some are as much as 200 years old. The walls of this 15th century church still bears traces of flames that were intended to bum out refugees during the Civil War.

The lychgate shown on the right is at the west corner of the churchyard. Timbers from the old belfry were used in its construction, and interesting carved bargeboards can be seen. For those exploring Painswick on foot, there is much to see in the town.

Painswick

All through history there has been. A trail of people who have done wrong in some way or another.

The punishment meted out was dependant on the severity of the crime. Some times prison was too severe for petty crimes and a cooling of fervour was all that was needed. 24 hours in the stocks was of course the ideal answer. The stocks shown in the sketch are called spectacle stocks because of their similarity in appearance to a pair of spectacles. This sample, possibly the only one in existence in this country, can be seen behind the wall on the north east corner of the Parish churchyard, Below is a sketch of Painswick Post office which is claimed by many as the oldest working Post Office in Britain. Painswick known as the Queen of the Cotswolds is a delightful Cotswold town nestling on the A46 Cheltenham to Stroud road.

Rodborough

At the most northernmost tip of Rodborough Common, 600ft above sea level stands Rodborough Fort pictured here below. Impressive as it is to look at, it is not unfortunately, a genuine medieval fort, being built in the last century. Rodborough Common, like the adjoining Minchinhampton Common, is almost exclusively National Trust Property, and lies in the southern confluence of the A46 and A419 at Stroud. Exciting views over the Stroud and Nailsworth Valleys are possible on fine days from both Commons. Walks, kite flying and picnics can be enjoyed and there is plenty of room for parking.

The Rollright Stones

The sketch of a single stone shown at the top of the following page is of a stone which stands nearly 9ft. high and is just over 5ft. wide. It is known as the King Stone and takes its place with two companion groups known as the Circle with seventy odd stones, and the Whispering Knights, a group of five some quarter of a mile away. These are collectively known as the famous Rollright Stones. The legend surrounding the stones is that a witch met a King and his army whose intention it was to rule all England. The witch, not being in favour of this, made a bargain with him, that he take seven long strides and 'if Long Compton thou cans't see, King of England thou shalt be'. Long Compton couldn't be seen from the seventh stride so the King, his men and the Whispering Knights were all turned to stone. So goes the legend, but in fact it is more likely to be as the little plaque describes in the front of the circle, a Late Neolithic or Bronze Age stone circle for ritual purposes which could date back some 4,000 years. It is for sure very old.

The Rollright Stones

Some amusement can be had trying to count the number of stones in the circle, partly shown at the bottom of this page as it is claimed that the same number can never be counted twice.

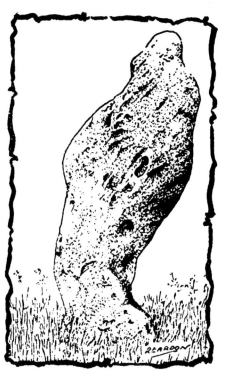

The stones are to be found just north of Chipping Norton by about three miles and to the west of the A34.

The Circle and the Whispering Knights are in Oxfordshire while just across the road the King Stone stands in Warwickshire. The little drawing below depicts a few of the stones in the circle looking west to east.

Long Compton lies about a mile to the north of the Rollright Stones.

Sapperton, Severn and Thames Canal

This canal was a project designed to enable conveyance of bulk goods from Bristol to London without making a coastal trip by sea. The canal ran from Framilode on the Severn to Lechlade on the Thames, a distance of 26 miles, and involved the construction of a tunnel from Sapperton, under Hailey Wood to Coates, 21 miles away. Built around 1785, it was later bought by the G.W.R. and closed in 1893. In 1911 the last boat went through the tunnel and the canal became derelict. The picture shows the Sapperton end of the tunnel, about 5 miles west of Cirencester just off the A419. For the boating enthusiast there has been a lot of discussion and to date some work has been carried out in an attempt to re open the canal and tunnel for leisure sailing.

Dipper

Kingfisher

Snowshill

The Village of Snowshill is a gem within a gem of a village as here can be found the world famous Snowshill Manor and found within the gardens of Snowshill Manor (NT) is presumably another example how St George and the Dragon features everywhere in the Cotswolds.

Southam, Leper Chute

The drawing to the right shows a leper chute, a protruding little structure not often seen in these times. This one can be seen on the wall of a fine tythe barn at Southam just north of Cheltenham off the A46 Winchcombe road. The reason for using a chute of this kind was that lepers could be given their ration of food without having to come into contact with their benefactor. The barn was used by monks for keeping sotres, and this gives rise to the thought that at one time there may have been a monastery or been a monastery or similar abbey at Southam.

South Cerney

At one time maybe better known for the airfield and RAF Station, South Cerney is fast becoming the "Water Sport Metropolis" of the Cotswolds. It has a wide variety of facilities laid on, even to giving sailing or water ski instruction. Situated just off the A419, the old Ermine Way, about 4 miles south of Cirencester, it is quite close to South Cerney. The village boasts a recorded history going back over 1000 years. The Church of All Hallows goes back to Norman times or earlier, but was altered considerably in the last century. Much of the old was incorporated with the new. At one time a farming community, South Cerney has undergone several changes in its local occupations, the Cotswold Marina being the latest. The picture above shows what is now a small folly, but may have previously been a windmill for corn grinding in the height of the farming era, between South Cerney and Siddington.

Stanway

To the right another St George and the Dragon, this time the war memorial near Stanway

GREAT CRESTED GREBE

Stow on the Wold

Stow on the Wold "where the wind blows cold", and at 800 feet above sea level this local saying can at times be very true, but cold or not, this town is a must for any visitor to the area. It has all the charms a Cotswold Town should have, from Town Square where the old town stocks stand, to Cotswold Church full of Civil War history. Stow figured in the 1642 1649 Civil War by St. Edward's Church being used for the prison of Sir Jacob Astley and about 1200 of his men in 1646.

The little sketch at the bottom left depicts not an entrance for a Hobbit, but the North door of St. Edward's Church.

A look about the town will show you a Lantern headed Market Cross recently restored that has been standing in the Square since about the 14th century.

While the sketch on the bottom right shows an archway leading into Church Street from an alley between St Edwards Church and the shops fronting onto Market Square.

North door

archway leading into Church Street

Stroud

An important centre since the middle of the 14th century for the weaving of cloth once made from the fleeces of Cotswold sheep, Stroud still has a number of mills working today.

Along the banks of the River Frome numerous factories and works will be found, many having connections with the cloth industry in some way. Famous for its good quality the material has a world wide demand. Industry is still expanding in and around the town today, but many are of modern variety.

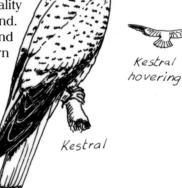

Kestral hovering

Kestral

Stroud also has its lighter side when work is done as can be seen pictured below this unusual inn sign spanning Union Street. It is unusual in that inn signs actually extending across streets like this could probably be counted on the fingers of one hand.

The town lies at the intersection of the Cheltenham to Bath road with the A419 Gloucester to Cirencester road.

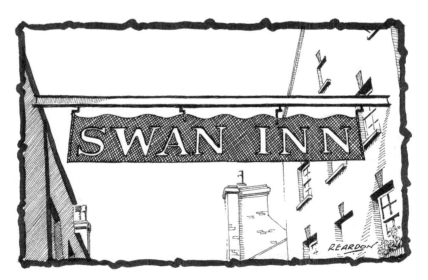

Sudeley Castle

Providing a wonderful day out with many exciting events taking place during the summer. The castle was once the home of Katherine Parr, the last wife of Henry VIII. Elizabeth 1 as a child lived at Sudeley and also the unfortunate Lady Jane Grey who accompanied Katherine Parr to Sudeley in the hope that she would marry Edward VI.

Sudeley Castle is one of the major attractions of the Cotswolds and is well worth a visit, the drawing below is of Vineyard Street leading to Sudeley.

'THE ROAD TO SUDELEY'
VINEYARD STREET, WINCHCOMBE, GLOS.

Teddington Hands

This is a stone with a canon ball hole in it at Teddington Hands, it is also known locally as the giants stone, the hole being the giants thumb print made when he throw it at Tewkesbury but he missed the town by many miles.

Tetbury

A small town, with a history going back to Saxon times. It owes most of its fine buildings to the great wool trade of the 15th and 16th centuries. The centre of the town is marked by the famous old Market House standing on twenty one pillars. Built in 1650, it was restored and altered in the early 1800's to much as it is today. The weathervane is interesting, being a pair of dolphins. Sheep might

This pump can be found not far from the centre of Tetbury

have been more in keeping with the times one would think. Not too big to walk round, there is much that can be seen of interest to those liking old buildings and architectural details. With the Market House at the centre of the town, Tetbury lies at the junction of the A433 from Cirencester and the B4014, Nailsworth to Malmesbury road.

Tewkesbury

A wonderful little town with its history going back to Norman times when the great Abbey of St. Mary the Virgin was built. The tower, the finest and largest Norman tower in the country, stands nearly 150 feet high. A look round this town will reveal many interesting  buildings, some that have figured in either true history or novels. On the east side of the A38, is the site of Margarets Camp, and at the end of Lower Lode Lane, on the left, is the Bloody Meadow both relics of the wars of the Roses 1445 85. The picture below shows a footbridge across the River Swilgate near Priors Park.

The Old Mill shown above featured as Abel Fletchers Mill in the novel "John Halifax, Gentleman" written by Mrs Craik.

Tewkesbury today is a busy and expanding town, with a big pleasure boating business and industry at nearby Newtown and Northway.

Tredington

To the right the Composite Tower and Spire are of the Little Church at Tredington and parts of this church date back to about 1100.

Upper Slaughter

Just a short walk from the well known Lower Slaughter you come to the sister village of Upper Slaughter pictured above and below.

THE PEACEFUL VILLAGE of UPPER SLAUGHTER, GLOUCESTERSHIRE

Willersey
A scene of tranquillity in the village of Willersey

A DELIGHTFUL SETTING AT WILLERSEY, IN WORCESTERSHIRE

Winchcombe
The little drawing on the right depicts the town clock in Winchcombe and may be seen in the High Street, on the front wall of the Town Hall, just a

few steps from Vineyard Street, and on the junction with North Street, the B4078. The clock was presented to the town by a very wealthy stockbroker, Mr. Reginald Prance, about 100 years ago. Mr. Prance, who lived at nearby Stanley Pontlarge, was an extremely benevolent citizen, at one time giving £70,000 to Tewkesbury Abbey among other notable public spirited deeds.

Winchcombe has a setting which obviously inspired people all through the ages to want to settle here. Two Roman villas to the south, an abbey at Hailes to the north east, Sudeley Castle to the south east, a hill fort about 3 miles to the south at Roel and a Stone Age burial chamber called Belas Knap on Cleeve Hill to the south.

Winchcombe

The old stocks pictured above in the little sketch may be seen in a small railed enclosure right at the road junction adjoining the Town Hall.

Located in the middle of a field on the west side of Hails Abbey, Winchcombe.

Some believe this 'structure' to be an old whipping post while others an ancient cross with the top part missing.

Winchcombe

The weird looking head is just one of many water chutes on
St Peters church in Winchcombe.

Wotton under Edge

One of the little old market towns that owes its share to the wool trade of the 15th to 16th century, Wotton has some very fine old buildings with something that will interest even the casual visitor. The present day Wotton Manor was built on the foundations of an earlier house which was sacked by Lord Berkeley's men in 1469. after about 30 years of intermittent feuding and bloodshed. On the corner of Market Street is the old Tolsey, with its very ornate clock, shown in the sketch to the left, protruding into the High Street. Above the clock face is a portrait of Queen Victoria flanked by the dates of succession to the throne in 1837 and Diamond Jubilee in 1897. The old Grammar School is one of the oldest seats of learning in the country, one of its scholars being Edward Jenner, famous for his discovery of vaccination. The Church of St. Mary has its features and is certainly worth a visit. Wotton under Edge lies on the B4058 Bristol to Nailsworth road at the junction with the B4060 Chipping Sodbury to Cam road.

Wyck Rissington

Pictured below the Green in the Village of Wyck Rissington

Wyck Rissington

The Church of St Lawrence at Wyck Rissington, Gloucestershire

The Duckpond and Green in Village of Wick Rissington in Gloucestershire

BV - #0050 - 210722 - C0 - 210/148/5 - PB - 9781901037098 - Gloss Lamination